FRESH LINES

A NETWORKER'S JOURNAL

 ISBN 978-1-3999-4452-6

WELCOME TO YOUR NETWORK JOURNAL

Hi, I'm James and I'm passionate about networking. I've been lucky enough to be part of incredible projects involving small businesses and global corporations alike. With networking constantly evolving, I created my own journal to keep all of my design ideas and troubleshooting notes in one neat, organised place and now I want to share it with you.

This journal can be a great resource for planning, organising, and documenting your thoughts and ideas. Some possible uses might include:

- Brainstorming: Use Fresh Lines to generate and record ideas for new networking projects or initiatives.
- Planning: Document your plans for implementing and managing your networking projects.
- Troubleshooting: Use your journal to document and track any issues or problems that arise in your networking projects, as well as your efforts to resolve them.
- Reflection: Make a note of the successes and challenges of your networking projects, and to identify areas for improvement. Write down your training and career goals in the back.

Overall, it can be a valuable tool for staying organised, keeping track of your progress, and continuously improving your networking skills and practices.

Each page includes a framework to create various designs and a dotted page for freeform notes. I especially like the subnet reference area. There's two examples to show you what's possible.

I'm looking forward to you making Fresh Lines part of your network journey.

Go make some Fresh Lines.

NETWORK JOURNAL

EXAMPLE

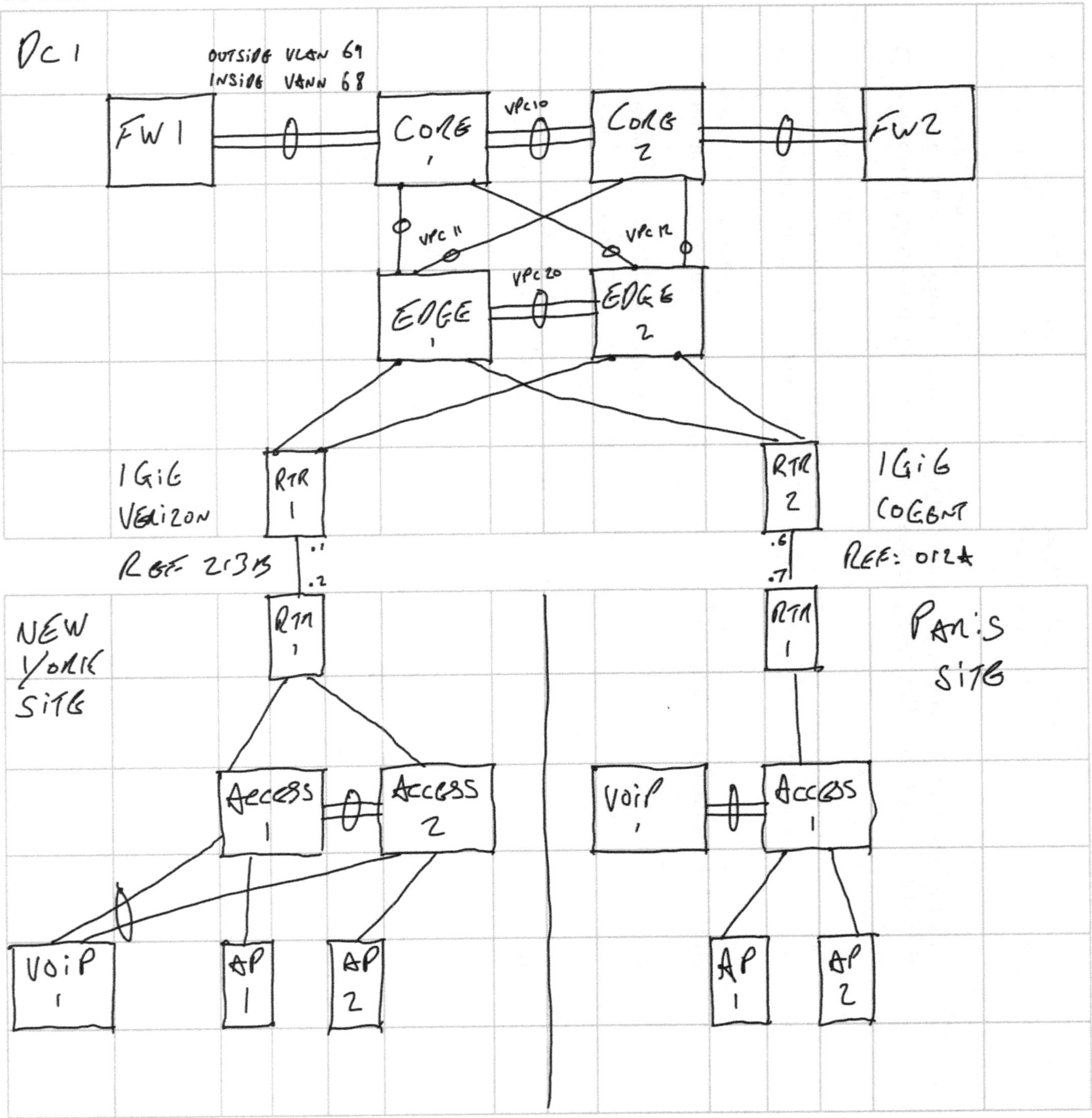

REFERENCE

CIDR	USABLE IP ADDRESSES	SUBNET MASK	WILDCARD MASK	BINARY
/30	2	255.255.255.252	0.0.0.3	11111000
/29	6	255.255.255.248	0.0.0.7	11110000
/28	14	255.255.255.240	0.0.0.15	11100000
/27	30	255.255.255.224	0.0.0.31	11000000
/26	62	255.255.255.192	0.0.0.63	11000000
/25	126	255.255.255.128	0.0.0.127	10000000
/24	254	255.255.255.0	0.0.0.255	00000000

	NETWORK	VLAN	VRF	FUNCTION
1	10.235.7.0/24	901	CORP_DATA_2	2ND FLOOR DATA
2	10.10.10.0/24	111	CORP_SRV	DC 1
3	10.162.10.0/24	21	—	New York
4	10.233.1.0/24	61	—	PARIS
5				
6				
7	10.111.103.0/30	9	WAN_NW	WAN 1
8	10.111.103.4/30	10	WAN_PRS	WAN 2
9				
10				

	FIREWALL	SOURCE	DESTINATION	TCP/ UDP PORT
1	INTERNET PERIMETER FW	10.235.7.0/24 10.236.79.0/24	188.235.7.199/32	TCP 443 UDP 4437
2	DC1_INET	10.162.10.0/24 10.233.1.0/24	8.8.8.8/32	UDP 53
3				
4				
5				
6				
7				
8				
9				
10				

NOTES

2x CORE 9300 - STACK KIT? - POWER?

IS 1GiG ENOUGH?

WHICH FIREWALL? CISCO, PALO OR CHECKPOINT?

1% Packet Loss Issue/Example

Circuits 1 Gig

London DC

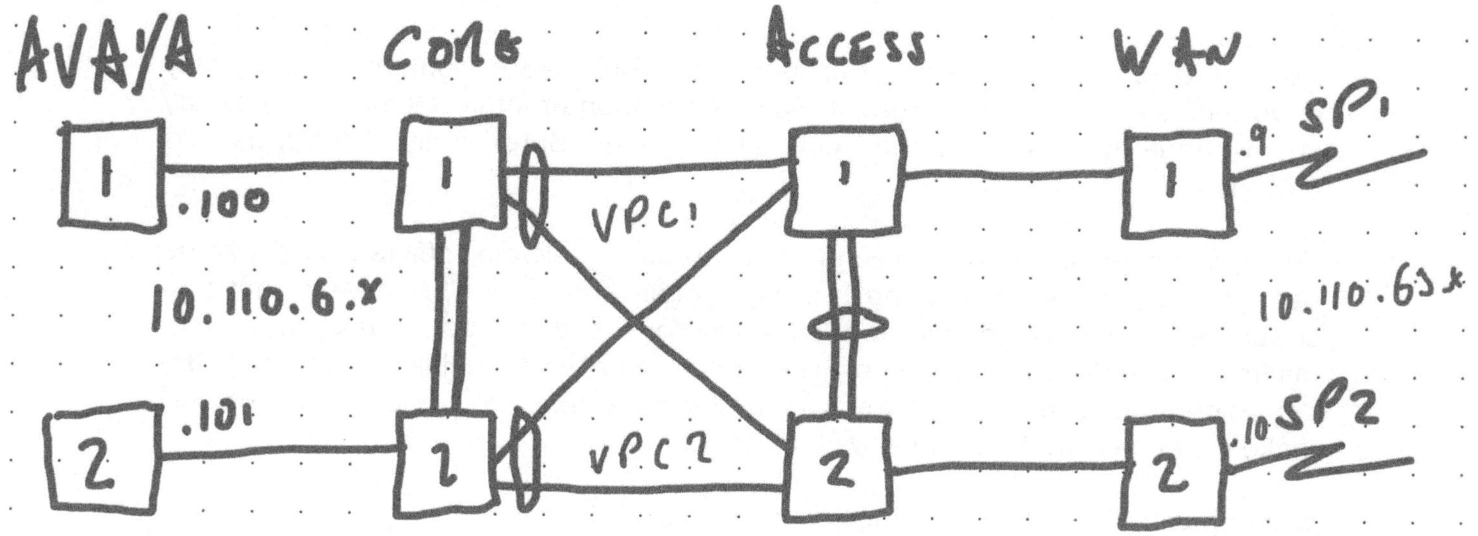

New York Office

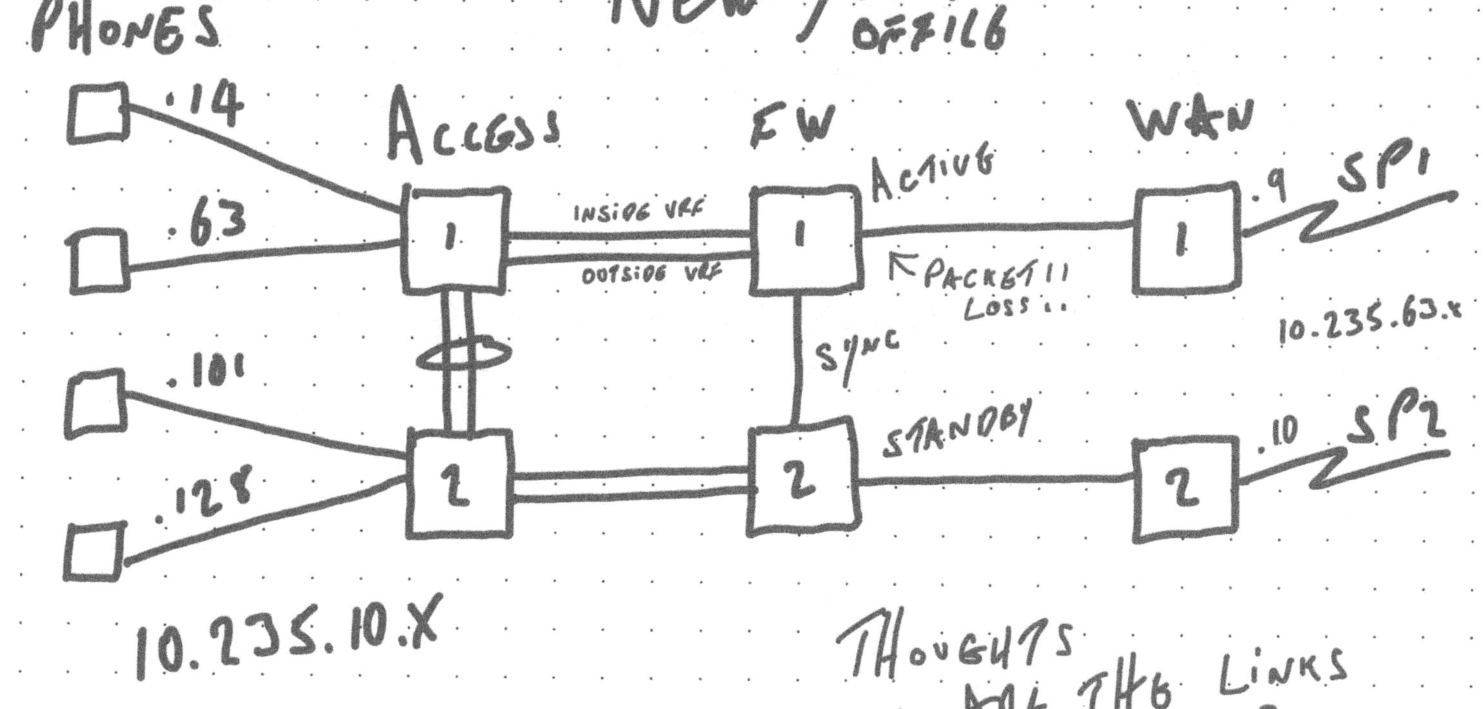

Thoughts

1. Are the links saturated?
2. Interface errors?
3. Flip firewall?

THE POWER OF SIMPLICITY

As you dive into designing your network, you'll learn something incredibly important: simpler is better. Sure, it may sound counter-intuitive...more complexity should equal more features and capabilities, right? Surprisingly, the opposite is actually true.

The goal of good network design is to create a reliable, efficient and secure network. So, focus on creating a clear, simple structure. This means that you should avoid overly complicated configurations and solutions. Instead, aim to minimise complexity and keep the design consistent. Make sure that the components of your network are well-defined and easy to understand. This will make it much easier to troubleshoot in the future.

Working with the right technologies and best practices, you can create a network that is robust and reliable. This will give you an edge over competitors who don't have a well-designed network.

In addition to keeping the design simple, you should also focus on creating a secure network. Security is an essential part of network design, as it helps to protect your data and ensure that only authorised users can access what they need. To make your network secure, use the latest security technologies, such as application aware firewalls, encryption and multi-factor authentication.

"GOOD DESIGN IS INTELLIGENCE MADE VISIBLE"

LE CORBUSIER

NETWORK DESIGN TECHNIQUES

There are several best practices for designing networks that can help ensure optimal performance, reliability, and security. Some of the key techniques to consider include:

- Hierarchical Network Design: This approach involves organising the network into layers, with each layer serving a specific function. This makes it easier to manage and troubleshoot, as well as to scale and expand the network as needed.
- Modular Network Design: This approach involves breaking the network down into smaller, independent units that can be easily added, removed, or modified without affecting the rest of the network. This makes it easier to maintain and update the network over time.
- Redundancy and High Availability: Ensuring that the network has redundant components and connections can help to improve its reliability and prevent outages. This can be achieved through the use of redundant switches, routers, and links, as well as protocols such as Hot Standby Router Protocol (HSRP) and Virtual Router Redundancy Protocol (VRRP).
- Network Segmentation: Segmenting the network into smaller, logical sub-networks can help to improve security and performance. This can be achieved through the use of VLANs, VRF's, access control lists (ACLs), and other security measures.
- Network Monitoring and Management: Regular monitoring and management of the network can help to identify and resolve issues before they become major problems. Tools such as Orion, Nagios, Cacti and Libre NMS can be used to monitor and manage the network. Daily config backups and good documentation will save you hours of pain in an outage situation.

DON'T FORGET ABOUT REAL-TIME APPS

I often see network designs that haven't taken real-time apps like VOIP and VIDEO into consideration. It's important to consider the bandwidth requirements and what is needed per user to ensure the network is able to support the desired number of users and the quality that is required.

The bandwidth requirements usually depend on a number of factors, including the following:

- The codec (coder-decoder) used to encode and decode the audio signals plays a major role in the bandwidth requirements of a VOIP system. Different codecs have different bandwidth requirements, with some using more bandwidth than others. G.729 and G.711 tend to be the most common ones used.

- The video quality settings can have a significant impact on the bandwidth requirements of a video conferencing system. Higher video quality settings will generally require more bandwidth.

- The number of users that will be using the VOIP / VIDEO system at the same time will affect the bandwidth requirements. The more users that are on the system, the more bandwidth will be required to support them.

In general, a VOIP system will require a minimum of **64 Kbps** (kilobits per second) of bandwidth per user for basic voice quality, and up to **128 Kbps** or more for high-quality audio.

Microsoft Teams recommends a minimum of **600 Kbps** of bandwidth per user for video calls, and up to **1.2 Mbps** (megabits per second) or more for high-quality video and audio. Zoom recommends a minimum of **1.5 Mbps** of bandwidth per user for video calls, and up to **2.5 Mbps** or more for high-quality video and audio. These bandwidth requirements may vary depending on the specific needs of the system.

QoS techniques can provide your network with the necessary support it needs to deliver a smooth and reliable experience. By prioritising traffic according to its importance, you can ensure that real-time apps are not affected by periods of congestion or other networking issues. This means that you can enjoy a consistent experience for all of your applications, no matter what challenges your network may face.

BENEFITS OF WELL-PLANNED IP ADDRESSING

IP addressing is a fundamental part of network design, allowing devices to communicate and access resources on the network. When designing an IP addressing scheme, several important factors come into play. You need to consider the size of the network, the number of hosts, the type of applications being used, and the type of addressing needed. Additionally, you'll need to keep in mind the physical layout of the network, the security requirements of the organisation, and any future growth that may be anticipated. With the right IP addressing scheme in place, you can ensure reliable and efficient communication across your network.

Keep these in mind:

- Network size: The number of devices and networks that will be connected to the network should be taken into account when designing the IP addressing scheme. This will help ensure that there are enough addresses available for all devices and networks.

- Network hierarchy: The network should be divided into logical subnets, with each subnet being assigned a range of IP addresses. This allows for better organisation and management of the network.

- Address assignment: IP addresses should be assigned to devices in a logical and consistent manner. This may include the use of static or dynamic address assignments, depending on the needs of the network.

- Address conservation: It is important to use IP addresses efficiently to ensure that the available address space is not exhausted. This may include the use of network address translation (NAT) or private IP addressing.

Designing an IP addressing scheme is not as intimidating as it may sound!

With careful planning, you can create an IP addressing scheme that effectively meets your organisation's needs.

So, let's get to designing!

MY TRAINING GOALS THIS YEAR

MY CAREER GOALS THIS YEAR

NETWORK

JOURNAL

REFERENCE

CIDR	USABLE IP'S	SUBNET	WILDCARD	BINARY
/30	2	255.255.255.252	0.0.0.3	11111100
/29	6	255.255.255.248	0.0.0.7	11111000
/28	14	255.255.255.240	0.0.0.15	11110000
/27	30	255.255.255.224	0.0.0.31	11100000
/26	62	255.255.255.192	0.0.0.63	11000000
/25	126	255.255.255.128	0.0.0.127	10000000
/24	254	255.255.255.0	0.0.0.255	00000000

	NETWORK	VLAN	VRF	FUNCTION
1				
2				
3				
4				
5				
6				
7				
8				
9				
10				

	FIREWALL / ZONE	SOURCE	DESTINATION	TCP/ UDP
1				
2				
3				
4				
5				
6				
7				
8				
9				
10				

NETWORK JOURNAL

REFERENCE

CIDR	USABLE IP'S	SUBNET	WILDCARD	BINARY
/30	2	255.255.255.252	0.0.0.3	11111100
/29	6	255.255.255.248	0.0.0.7	11111000
/28	14	255.255.255.240	0.0.0.15	11110000
/27	30	255.255.255.224	0.0.0.31	11100000
/26	62	255.255.255.192	0.0.0.63	11000000
/25	126	255.255.255.128	0.0.0.127	10000000
/24	254	255.255.255.0	0.0.0.255	00000000

	NETWORK	VLAN	VRF	FUNCTION
1				
2				
3				
4				
5				
6				
7				
8				
9				
10				

	FIREWALL / ZONE	SOURCE	DESTINATION	TCP/ UDP
1				
2				
3				
4				
5				
6				
7				
8				
9				
10				

NETWORK

JOURNAL

REFERENCE

CIDR	USABLE IP'S	SUBNET	WILDCARD	BINARY
/30	2	255.255.255.252	0.0.0.3	11111100
/29	6	255.255.255.248	0.0.0.7	11111000
/28	14	255.255.255.240	0.0.0.15	11110000
/27	30	255.255.255.224	0.0.0.31	11100000
/26	62	255.255.255.192	0.0.0.63	11000000
/25	126	255.255.255.128	0.0.0.127	10000000
/24	254	255.255.255.0	0.0.0.255	00000000

	NETWORK	VLAN	VRF	FUNCTION
1				
2				
3				
4				
5				
6				
7				
8				
9				
10				

	FIREWALL / ZONE	SOURCE	DESTINATION	TCP/ UDP
1				
2				
3				
4				
5				
6				
7				
8				
9				
10				

NETWORK

JOURNAL

REFERENCE

CIDR	USABLE IP'S	SUBNET	WILDCARD	BINARY
/30	2	255.255.255.252	0.0.0.3	11111100
/29	6	255.255.255.248	0.0.0.7	11111000
/28	14	255.255.255.240	0.0.0.15	11110000
/27	30	255.255.255.224	0.0.0.31	11100000
/26	62	255.255.255.192	0.0.0.63	11000000
/25	126	255.255.255.128	0.0.0.127	10000000
/24	254	255.255.255.0	0.0.0.255	00000000

	NETWORK	VLAN	VRF	FUNCTION
1				
2				
3				
4				
5				
6				
7				
8				
9				
10				

	FIREWALL / ZONE	SOURCE	DESTINATION	TCP/ UDP
1				
2				
3				
4				
5				
6				
7				
8				
9				
10				

NETWORK

JOURNAL

REFERENCE

CIDR	USABLE IP'S	SUBNET	WILDCARD	BINARY
/30	2	255.255.255.252	0.0.0.3	11111100
/29	6	255.255.255.248	0.0.0.7	11111000
/28	14	255.255.255.240	0.0.0.15	11110000
/27	30	255.255.255.224	0.0.0.31	11100000
/26	62	255.255.255.192	0.0.0.63	11000000
/25	126	255.255.255.128	0.0.0.127	10000000
/24	254	255.255.255.0	0.0.0.255	00000000

	NETWORK	VLAN	VRF	FUNCTION
1				
2				
3				
4				
5				
6				
7				
8				
9				
10				

	FIREWALL / ZONE	SOURCE	DESTINATION	TCP/ UDP
1				
2				
3				
4				
5				
6				
7				
8				
9				
10				

NETWORK JOURNAL

REFERENCE

CIDR	USABLE IP'S	SUBNET	WILDCARD	BINARY
/30	2	255.255.255.252	0.0.0.3	11111100
/29	6	255.255.255.248	0.0.0.7	11111000
/28	14	255.255.255.240	0.0.0.15	11110000
/27	30	255.255.255.224	0.0.0.31	11100000
/26	62	255.255.255.192	0.0.0.63	11000000
/25	126	255.255.255.128	0.0.0.127	10000000
/24	254	255.255.255.0	0.0.0.255	00000000

	NETWORK	VLAN	VRF	FUNCTION
1				
2				
3				
4				
5				
6				
7				
8				
9				
10				

	FIREWALL / ZONE	SOURCE	DESTINATION	TCP/ UDP
1				
2				
3				
4				
5				
6				
7				
8				
9				
10				

NETWORK ______________________

JOURNAL

REFERENCE

CIDR	USABLE IP'S	SUBNET	WILDCARD	BINARY
/30	2	255.255.255.252	0.0.0.3	11111100
/29	6	255.255.255.248	0.0.0.7	11111000
/28	14	255.255.255.240	0.0.0.15	11110000
/27	30	255.255.255.224	0.0.0.31	11100000
/26	62	255.255.255.192	0.0.0.63	11000000
/25	126	255.255.255.128	0.0.0.127	10000000
/24	254	255.255.255.0	0.0.0.255	00000000

	NETWORK	VLAN	VRF	FUNCTION
1				
2				
3				
4				
5				
6				
7				
8				
9				
10				

	FIREWALL / ZONE	SOURCE	DESTINATION	TCP/ UDP
1				
2				
3				
4				
5				
6				
7				
8				
9				
10				

NETWORK JOURNAL

REFERENCE

CIDR	USABLE IP'S	SUBNET	WILDCARD	BINARY
/30	2	255.255.255.252	0.0.0.3	11111100
/29	6	255.255.255.248	0.0.0.7	11111000
/28	14	255.255.255.240	0.0.0.15	11110000
/27	30	255.255.255.224	0.0.0.31	11100000
/26	62	255.255.255.192	0.0.0.63	11000000
/25	126	255.255.255.128	0.0.0.127	10000000
/24	254	255.255.255.0	0.0.0.255	00000000

	NETWORK	VLAN	VRF	FUNCTION
1				
2				
3				
4				
5				
6				
7				
8				
9				
10				

	FIREWALL / ZONE	SOURCE	DESTINATION	TCP/ UDP
1				
2				
3				
4				
5				
6				
7				
8				
9				
10				

NETWORK JOURNAL

REFERENCE

CIDR	USABLE IP'S	SUBNET	WILDCARD	BINARY
/30	2	255.255.255.252	0.0.0.3	11111100
/29	6	255.255.255.248	0.0.0.7	11111000
/28	14	255.255.255.240	0.0.0.15	11110000
/27	30	255.255.255.224	0.0.0.31	11100000
/26	62	255.255.255.192	0.0.0.63	11000000
/25	126	255.255.255.128	0.0.0.127	10000000
/24	254	255.255.255.0	0.0.0.255	00000000

	NETWORK	VLAN	VRF	FUNCTION
1				
2				
3				
4				
5				
6				
7				
8				
9				
10				

	FIREWALL / ZONE	SOURCE	DESTINATION	TCP/ UDP
1				
2				
3				
4				
5				
6				
7				
8				
9				
10				

NETWORK

JOURNAL

REFERENCE

CIDR	USABLE IP'S	SUBNET	WILDCARD	BINARY
/30	2	255.255.255.252	0.0.0.3	11111100
/29	6	255.255.255.248	0.0.0.7	11111000
/28	14	255.255.255.240	0.0.0.15	11110000
/27	30	255.255.255.224	0.0.0.31	11100000
/26	62	255.255.255.192	0.0.0.63	11000000
/25	126	255.255.255.128	0.0.0.127	10000000
/24	254	255.255.255.0	0.0.0.255	00000000

	NETWORK	VLAN	VRF	FUNCTION
1				
2				
3				
4				
5				
6				
7				
8				
9				
10				

	FIREWALL / ZONE	SOURCE	DESTINATION	TCP/ UDP
1				
2				
3				
4				
5				
6				
7				
8				
9				
10				

NETWORK JOURNAL

REFERENCE

CIDR	USABLE IP'S	SUBNET	WILDCARD	BINARY
/30	2	255.255.255.252	0.0.0.3	11111100
/29	6	255.255.255.248	0.0.0.7	11111000
/28	14	255.255.255.240	0.0.0.15	11110000
/27	30	255.255.255.224	0.0.0.31	11100000
/26	62	255.255.255.192	0.0.0.63	11000000
/25	126	255.255.255.128	0.0.0.127	10000000
/24	254	255.255.255.0	0.0.0.255	00000000

	NETWORK	VLAN	VRF	FUNCTION
1				
2				
3				
4				
5				
6				
7				
8				
9				
10				

	FIREWALL / ZONE	SOURCE	DESTINATION	TCP/ UDP
1				
2				
3				
4				
5				
6				
7				
8				
9				
10				

NETWORK ____________________

JOURNAL

REFERENCE

CIDR	USABLE IP'S	SUBNET	WILDCARD	BINARY
/30	2	255.255.255.252	0.0.0.3	11111100
/29	6	255.255.255.248	0.0.0.7	11111000
/28	14	255.255.255.240	0.0.0.15	11110000
/27	30	255.255.255.224	0.0.0.31	11100000
/26	62	255.255.255.192	0.0.0.63	11000000
/25	126	255.255.255.128	0.0.0.127	10000000
/24	254	255.255.255.0	0.0.0.255	00000000

	NETWORK	VLAN	VRF	FUNCTION
1				
2				
3				
4				
5				
6				
7				
8				
9				
10				

	FIREWALL / ZONE	SOURCE	DESTINATION	TCP/ UDP
1				
2				
3				
4				
5				
6				
7				
8				
9				
10				

NETWORK JOURNAL

REFERENCE

CIDR	USABLE IP'S	SUBNET	WILDCARD	BINARY
/30	2	255.255.255.252	0.0.0.3	11111100
/29	6	255.255.255.248	0.0.0.7	11111000
/28	14	255.255.255.240	0.0.0.15	11110000
/27	30	255.255.255.224	0.0.0.31	11100000
/26	62	255.255.255.192	0.0.0.63	11000000
/25	126	255.255.255.128	0.0.0.127	10000000
/24	254	255.255.255.0	0.0.0.255	00000000

	NETWORK	VLAN	VRF	FUNCTION
1				
2				
3				
4				
5				
6				
7				
8				
9				
10				

	FIREWALL / ZONE	SOURCE	DESTINATION	TCP/ UDP
1				
2				
3				
4				
5				
6				
7				
8				
9				
10				

NETWORK

JOURNAL

REFERENCE

CIDR	USABLE IP'S	SUBNET	WILDCARD	BINARY
/30	2	255.255.255.252	0.0.0.3	11111100
/29	6	255.255.255.248	0.0.0.7	11111000
/28	14	255.255.255.240	0.0.0.15	11110000
/27	30	255.255.255.224	0.0.0.31	11100000
/26	62	255.255.255.192	0.0.0.63	11000000
/25	126	255.255.255.128	0.0.0.127	10000000
/24	254	255.255.255.0	0.0.0.255	00000000

	NETWORK	VLAN	VRF	FUNCTION
1				
2				
3				
4				
5				
6				
7				
8				
9				
10				

	FIREWALL / ZONE	SOURCE	DESTINATION	TCP/ UDP
1				
2				
3				
4				
5				
6				
7				
8				
9				
10				

NETWORK

JOURNAL

REFERENCE

CIDR	USABLE IP'S	SUBNET	WILDCARD	BINARY
/30	2	255.255.255.252	0.0.0.3	11111100
/29	6	255.255.255.248	0.0.0.7	11111000
/28	14	255.255.255.240	0.0.0.15	11110000
/27	30	255.255.255.224	0.0.0.31	11100000
/26	62	255.255.255.192	0.0.0.63	11000000
/25	126	255.255.255.128	0.0.0.127	10000000
/24	254	255.255.255.0	0.0.0.255	00000000

	NETWORK	VLAN	VRF	FUNCTION
1				
2				
3				
4				
5				
6				
7				
8				
9				
10				

	FIREWALL / ZONE	SOURCE	DESTINATION	TCP/ UDP
1				
2				
3				
4				
5				
6				
7				
8				
9				
10				

NETWORK
JOURNAL

REFERENCE

CIDR	USABLE IP'S	SUBNET	WILDCARD	BINARY
/30	2	255.255.255.252	0.0.0.3	11111100
/29	6	255.255.255.248	0.0.0.7	11111000
/28	14	255.255.255.240	0.0.0.15	11110000
/27	30	255.255.255.224	0.0.0.31	11100000
/26	62	255.255.255.192	0.0.0.63	11000000
/25	126	255.255.255.128	0.0.0.127	10000000
/24	254	255.255.255.0	0.0.0.255	00000000

	NETWORK	VLAN	VRF	FUNCTION
1				
2				
3				
4				
5				
6				
7				
8				
9				
10				

	FIREWALL / ZONE	SOURCE	DESTINATION	TCP/ UDP
1				
2				
3				
4				
5				
6				
7				
8				
9				
10				

NETWORK JOURNAL

REFERENCE

CIDR	USABLE IP'S	SUBNET	WILDCARD	BINARY
/30	2	255.255.255.252	0.0.0.3	11111100
/29	6	255.255.255.248	0.0.0.7	11111000
/28	14	255.255.255.240	0.0.0.15	11110000
/27	30	255.255.255.224	0.0.0.31	11100000
/26	62	255.255.255.192	0.0.0.63	11000000
/25	126	255.255.255.128	0.0.0.127	10000000
/24	254	255.255.255.0	0.0.0.255	00000000

	NETWORK	VLAN	VRF	FUNCTION
1				
2				
3				
4				
5				
6				
7				
8				
9				
10				

	FIREWALL / ZONE	SOURCE	DESTINATION	TCP/ UDP
1				
2				
3				
4				
5				
6				
7				
8				
9				
10				

NETWORK

JOURNAL

REFERENCE

CIDR	USABLE IP'S	SUBNET	WILDCARD	BINARY
/30	2	255.255.255.252	0.0.0.3	11111100
/29	6	255.255.255.248	0.0.0.7	11111000
/28	14	255.255.255.240	0.0.0.15	11110000
/27	30	255.255.255.224	0.0.0.31	11100000
/26	62	255.255.255.192	0.0.0.63	11000000
/25	126	255.255.255.128	0.0.0.127	10000000
/24	254	255.255.255.0	0.0.0.255	00000000

	NETWORK	VLAN	VRF	FUNCTION
1				
2				
3				
4				
5				
6				
7				
8				
9				
10				

	FIREWALL / ZONE	SOURCE	DESTINATION	TCP/ UDP
1				
2				
3				
4				
5				
6				
7				
8				
9				
10				

NETWORK

JOURNAL

REFERENCE

CIDR	USABLE IP'S	SUBNET	WILDCARD	BINARY
/30	2	255.255.255.252	0.0.0.3	11111100
/29	6	255.255.255.248	0.0.0.7	11111000
/28	14	255.255.255.240	0.0.0.15	11110000
/27	30	255.255.255.224	0.0.0.31	11100000
/26	62	255.255.255.192	0.0.0.63	11000000
/25	126	255.255.255.128	0.0.0.127	10000000
/24	254	255.255.255.0	0.0.0.255	00000000

	NETWORK	VLAN	VRF	FUNCTION
1				
2				
3				
4				
5				
6				
7				
8				
9				
10				

	FIREWALL / ZONE	SOURCE	DESTINATION	TCP/ UDP
1				
2				
3				
4				
5				
6				
7				
8				
9				
10				

NETWORK JOURNAL

REFERENCE

CIDR	USABLE IP'S	SUBNET	WILDCARD	BINARY
/30	2	255.255.255.252	0.0.0.3	11111100
/29	6	255.255.255.248	0.0.0.7	11111000
/28	14	255.255.255.240	0.0.0.15	11110000
/27	30	255.255.255.224	0.0.0.31	11100000
/26	62	255.255.255.192	0.0.0.63	11000000
/25	126	255.255.255.128	0.0.0.127	10000000
/24	254	255.255.255.0	0.0.0.255	00000000

	NETWORK	VLAN	VRF	FUNCTION
1				
2				
3				
4				
5				
6				
7				
8				
9				
10				

	FIREWALL / ZONE	SOURCE	DESTINATION	TCP/ UDP
1				
2				
3				
4				
5				
6				
7				
8				
9				
10				

NETWORK JOURNAL

REFERENCE

CIDR	USABLE IP'S	SUBNET	WILDCARD	BINARY
/30	2	255.255.255.252	0.0.0.3	11111100
/29	6	255.255.255.248	0.0.0.7	11111000
/28	14	255.255.255.240	0.0.0.15	11110000
/27	30	255.255.255.224	0.0.0.31	11100000
/26	62	255.255.255.192	0.0.0.63	11000000
/25	126	255.255.255.128	0.0.0.127	10000000
/24	254	255.255.255.0	0.0.0.255	00000000

	NETWORK	VLAN	VRF	FUNCTION
1				
2				
3				
4				
5				
6				
7				
8				
9				
10				

	FIREWALL / ZONE	SOURCE	DESTINATION	TCP/ UDP
1				
2				
3				
4				
5				
6				
7				
8				
9				
10				

NETWORK JOURNAL

REFERENCE

CIDR	USABLE IP'S	SUBNET	WILDCARD	BINARY
/30	2	255.255.255.252	0.0.0.3	11111100
/29	6	255.255.255.248	0.0.0.7	11111000
/28	14	255.255.255.240	0.0.0.15	11110000
/27	30	255.255.255.224	0.0.0.31	11100000
/26	62	255.255.255.192	0.0.0.63	11000000
/25	126	255.255.255.128	0.0.0.127	10000000
/24	254	255.255.255.0	0.0.0.255	00000000

	NETWORK	VLAN	VRF	FUNCTION
1				
2				
3				
4				
5				
6				
7				
8				
9				
10				

	FIREWALL / ZONE	SOURCE	DESTINATION	TCP/ UDP
1				
2				
3				
4				
5				
6				
7				
8				
9				
10				

NETWORK JOURNAL

REFERENCE

CIDR	USABLE IP'S	SUBNET	WILDCARD	BINARY
/30	2	255.255.255.252	0.0.0.3	11111100
/29	6	255.255.255.248	0.0.0.7	11111000
/28	14	255.255.255.240	0.0.0.15	11110000
/27	30	255.255.255.224	0.0.0.31	11100000
/26	62	255.255.255.192	0.0.0.63	11000000
/25	126	255.255.255.128	0.0.0.127	10000000
/24	254	255.255.255.0	0.0.0.255	00000000

	NETWORK	VLAN	VRF	FUNCTION
1				
2				
3				
4				
5				
6				
7				
8				
9				
10				

	FIREWALL / ZONE	SOURCE	DESTINATION	TCP/ UDP
1				
2				
3				
4				
5				
6				
7				
8				
9				
10				

NETWORK
JOURNAL

REFERENCE

CIDR	USABLE IP'S	SUBNET	WILDCARD	BINARY
/30	2	255.255.255.252	0.0.0.3	11111100
/29	6	255.255.255.248	0.0.0.7	11111000
/28	14	255.255.255.240	0.0.0.15	11110000
/27	30	255.255.255.224	0.0.0.31	11100000
/26	62	255.255.255.192	0.0.0.63	11000000
/25	126	255.255.255.128	0.0.0.127	10000000
/24	254	255.255.255.0	0.0.0.255	00000000

	NETWORK	VLAN	VRF	FUNCTION
1				
2				
3				
4				
5				
6				
7				
8				
9				
10				

	FIREWALL / ZONE	SOURCE	DESTINATION	TCP/ UDP
1				
2				
3				
4				
5				
6				
7				
8				
9				
10				

NETWORK JOURNAL

REFERENCE

CIDR	USABLE IP'S	SUBNET	WILDCARD	BINARY
/30	2	255.255.255.252	0.0.0.3	11111100
/29	6	255.255.255.248	0.0.0.7	11111000
/28	14	255.255.255.240	0.0.0.15	11110000
/27	30	255.255.255.224	0.0.0.31	11100000
/26	62	255.255.255.192	0.0.0.63	11000000
/25	126	255.255.255.128	0.0.0.127	10000000
/24	254	255.255.255.0	0.0.0.255	00000000

	NETWORK	VLAN	VRF	FUNCTION
1				
2				
3				
4				
5				
6				
7				
8				
9				
10				

	FIREWALL / ZONE	SOURCE	DESTINATION	TCP/ UDP
1				
2				
3				
4				
5				
6				
7				
8				
9				
10				

NETWORK JOURNAL

REFERENCE

CIDR	USABLE IP'S	SUBNET	WILDCARD	BINARY
/30	2	255.255.255.252	0.0.0.3	11111100
/29	6	255.255.255.248	0.0.0.7	11111000
/28	14	255.255.255.240	0.0.0.15	11110000
/27	30	255.255.255.224	0.0.0.31	11100000
/26	62	255.255.255.192	0.0.0.63	11000000
/25	126	255.255.255.128	0.0.0.127	10000000
/24	254	255.255.255.0	0.0.0.255	00000000

	NETWORK	VLAN	VRF	FUNCTION
1				
2				
3				
4				
5				
6				
7				
8				
9				
10				

	FIREWALL / ZONE	SOURCE	DESTINATION	TCP/ UDP
1				
2				
3				
4				
5				
6				
7				
8				
9				
10				

NETWORK JOURNAL

REFERENCE

CIDR	USABLE IP'S	SUBNET	WILDCARD	BINARY
/30	2	255.255.255.252	0.0.0.3	11111100
/29	6	255.255.255.248	0.0.0.7	11111000
/28	14	255.255.255.240	0.0.0.15	11110000
/27	30	255.255.255.224	0.0.0.31	11100000
/26	62	255.255.255.192	0.0.0.63	11000000
/25	126	255.255.255.128	0.0.0.127	10000000
/24	254	255.255.255.0	0.0.0.255	00000000

	NETWORK	VLAN	VRF	FUNCTION
1				
2				
3				
4				
5				
6				
7				
8				
9				
10				

	FIREWALL / ZONE	SOURCE	DESTINATION	TCP/ UDP
1				
2				
3				
4				
5				
6				
7				
8				
9				
10				

NETWORK

JOURNAL

REFERENCE

CIDR	USABLE IP'S	SUBNET	WILDCARD	BINARY
/30	2	255.255.255.252	0.0.0.3	11111100
/29	6	255.255.255.248	0.0.0.7	11111000
/28	14	255.255.255.240	0.0.0.15	11110000
/27	30	255.255.255.224	0.0.0.31	11100000
/26	62	255.255.255.192	0.0.0.63	11000000
/25	126	255.255.255.128	0.0.0.127	10000000
/24	254	255.255.255.0	0.0.0.255	00000000

	NETWORK	VLAN	VRF	FUNCTION
1				
2				
3				
4				
5				
6				
7				
8				
9				
10				

	FIREWALL / ZONE	SOURCE	DESTINATION	TCP/ UDP
1				
2				
3				
4				
5				
6				
7				
8				
9				
10				

NETWORK JOURNAL

REFERENCE

CIDR	USABLE IP'S	SUBNET	WILDCARD	BINARY
/30	2	255.255.255.252	0.0.0.3	11111100
/29	6	255.255.255.248	0.0.0.7	11111000
/28	14	255.255.255.240	0.0.0.15	11110000
/27	30	255.255.255.224	0.0.0.31	11100000
/26	62	255.255.255.192	0.0.0.63	11000000
/25	126	255.255.255.128	0.0.0.127	10000000
/24	254	255.255.255.0	0.0.0.255	00000000

	NETWORK	VLAN	VRF	FUNCTION
1				
2				
3				
4				
5				
6				
7				
8				
9				
10				

	FIREWALL / ZONE	SOURCE	DESTINATION	TCP/ UDP
1				
2				
3				
4				
5				
6				
7				
8				
9				
10				

NETWORK

JOURNAL

REFERENCE

CIDR	USABLE IP'S	SUBNET	WILDCARD	BINARY
/30	2	255.255.255.252	0.0.0.3	11111100
/29	6	255.255.255.248	0.0.0.7	11111000
/28	14	255.255.255.240	0.0.0.15	11110000
/27	30	255.255.255.224	0.0.0.31	11100000
/26	62	255.255.255.192	0.0.0.63	11000000
/25	126	255.255.255.128	0.0.0.127	10000000
/24	254	255.255.255.0	0.0.0.255	00000000

	NETWORK	VLAN	VRF	FUNCTION
1				
2				
3				
4				
5				
6				
7				
8				
9				
10				

	FIREWALL / ZONE	SOURCE	DESTINATION	TCP/ UDP
1				
2				
3				
4				
5				
6				
7				
8				
9				
10				

NETWORK JOURNAL

REFERENCE

CIDR	USABLE IP'S	SUBNET	WILDCARD	BINARY
/30	2	255.255.255.252	0.0.0.3	11111100
/29	6	255.255.255.248	0.0.0.7	11111000
/28	14	255.255.255.240	0.0.0.15	11110000
/27	30	255.255.255.224	0.0.0.31	11100000
/26	62	255.255.255.192	0.0.0.63	11000000
/25	126	255.255.255.128	0.0.0.127	10000000
/24	254	255.255.255.0	0.0.0.255	00000000

	NETWORK	VLAN	VRF	FUNCTION
1				
2				
3				
4				
5				
6				
7				
8				
9				
10				

	FIREWALL / ZONE	SOURCE	DESTINATION	TCP/ UDP
1				
2				
3				
4				
5				
6				
7				
8				
9				
10				

NETWORK JOURNAL

REFERENCE

CIDR	USABLE IP'S	SUBNET	WILDCARD	BINARY
/30	2	255.255.255.252	0.0.0.3	11111100
/29	6	255.255.255.248	0.0.0.7	11111000
/28	14	255.255.255.240	0.0.0.15	11110000
/27	30	255.255.255.224	0.0.0.31	11100000
/26	62	255.255.255.192	0.0.0.63	11000000
/25	126	255.255.255.128	0.0.0.127	10000000
/24	254	255.255.255.0	0.0.0.255	00000000

	NETWORK	VLAN	VRF	FUNCTION
1				
2				
3				
4				
5				
6				
7				
8				
9				
10				

	FIREWALL / ZONE	SOURCE	DESTINATION	TCP/ UDP
1				
2				
3				
4				
5				
6				
7				
8				
9				
10				

NETWORK JOURNAL

REFERENCE

CIDR	USABLE IP'S	SUBNET	WILDCARD	BINARY
/30	2	255.255.255.252	0.0.0.3	11111100
/29	6	255.255.255.248	0.0.0.7	11111000
/28	14	255.255.255.240	0.0.0.15	11110000
/27	30	255.255.255.224	0.0.0.31	11100000
/26	62	255.255.255.192	0.0.0.63	11000000
/25	126	255.255.255.128	0.0.0.127	10000000
/24	254	255.255.255.0	0.0.0.255	00000000

	NETWORK	VLAN	VRF	FUNCTION
1				
2				
3				
4				
5				
6				
7				
8				
9				
10				

	FIREWALL / ZONE	SOURCE	DESTINATION	TCP/ UDP
1				
2				
3				
4				
5				
6				
7				
8				
9				
10				

NETWORK JOURNAL

REFERENCE

CIDR	USABLE IP'S	SUBNET	WILDCARD	BINARY
/30	2	255.255.255.252	0.0.0.3	11111100
/29	6	255.255.255.248	0.0.0.7	11111000
/28	14	255.255.255.240	0.0.0.15	11110000
/27	30	255.255.255.224	0.0.0.31	11100000
/26	62	255.255.255.192	0.0.0.63	11000000
/25	126	255.255.255.128	0.0.0.127	10000000
/24	254	255.255.255.0	0.0.0.255	00000000

	NETWORK	VLAN	VRF	FUNCTION
1				
2				
3				
4				
5				
6				
7				
8				
9				
10				

	FIREWALL / ZONE	SOURCE	DESTINATION	TCP/ UDP
1				
2				
3				
4				
5				
6				
7				
8				
9				
10				

NETWORK

JOURNAL

REFERENCE

CIDR	USABLE IP'S	SUBNET	WILDCARD	BINARY
/30	2	255.255.255.252	0.0.0.3	11111100
/29	6	255.255.255.248	0.0.0.7	11111000
/28	14	255.255.255.240	0.0.0.15	11110000
/27	30	255.255.255.224	0.0.0.31	11100000
/26	62	255.255.255.192	0.0.0.63	11000000
/25	126	255.255.255.128	0.0.0.127	10000000
/24	254	255.255.255.0	0.0.0.255	00000000

	NETWORK	VLAN	VRF	FUNCTION
1				
2				
3				
4				
5				
6				
7				
8				
9				
10				

	FIREWALL / ZONE	SOURCE	DESTINATION	TCP/ UDP
1				
2				
3				
4				
5				
6				
7				
8				
9				
10				

NETWORK

JOURNAL

REFERENCE

CIDR	USABLE IP'S	SUBNET	WILDCARD	BINARY
/30	2	255.255.255.252	0.0.0.3	11111100
/29	6	255.255.255.248	0.0.0.7	11111000
/28	14	255.255.255.240	0.0.0.15	11110000
/27	30	255.255.255.224	0.0.0.31	11100000
/26	62	255.255.255.192	0.0.0.63	11000000
/25	126	255.255.255.128	0.0.0.127	10000000
/24	254	255.255.255.0	0.0.0.255	00000000

	NETWORK	VLAN	VRF	FUNCTION
1				
2				
3				
4				
5				
6				
7				
8				
9				
10				

	FIREWALL / ZONE	SOURCE	DESTINATION	TCP/ UDP
1				
2				
3				
4				
5				
6				
7				
8				
9				
10				

NETWORK JOURNAL

REFERENCE

CIDR	USABLE IP'S	SUBNET	WILDCARD	BINARY
/30	2	255.255.255.252	0.0.0.3	11111100
/29	6	255.255.255.248	0.0.0.7	11111000
/28	14	255.255.255.240	0.0.0.15	11110000
/27	30	255.255.255.224	0.0.0.31	11100000
/26	62	255.255.255.192	0.0.0.63	11000000
/25	126	255.255.255.128	0.0.0.127	10000000
/24	254	255.255.255.0	0.0.0.255	00000000

	NETWORK	VLAN	VRF	FUNCTION
1				
2				
3				
4				
5				
6				
7				
8				
9				
10				

	FIREWALL / ZONE	SOURCE	DESTINATION	TCP/ UDP
1				
2				
3				
4				
5				
6				
7				
8				
9				
10				

NETWORK ____________________

JOURNAL

REFERENCE

CIDR	USABLE IP'S	SUBNET	WILDCARD	BINARY
/30	2	255.255.255.252	0.0.0.3	11111100
/29	6	255.255.255.248	0.0.0.7	11111000
/28	14	255.255.255.240	0.0.0.15	11110000
/27	30	255.255.255.224	0.0.0.31	11100000
/26	62	255.255.255.192	0.0.0.63	11000000
/25	126	255.255.255.128	0.0.0.127	10000000
/24	254	255.255.255.0	0.0.0.255	00000000

	NETWORK	VLAN	VRF	FUNCTION
1				
2				
3				
4				
5				
6				
7				
8				
9				
10				

	FIREWALL / ZONE	SOURCE	DESTINATION	TCP/ UDP
1				
2				
3				
4				
5				
6				
7				
8				
9				
10				

NETWORK

JOURNAL

REFERENCE

CIDR	USABLE IP'S	SUBNET	WILDCARD	BINARY
/30	2	255.255.255.252	0.0.0.3	11111100
/29	6	255.255.255.248	0.0.0.7	11111000
/28	14	255.255.255.240	0.0.0.15	11110000
/27	30	255.255.255.224	0.0.0.31	11100000
/26	62	255.255.255.192	0.0.0.63	11000000
/25	126	255.255.255.128	0.0.0.127	10000000
/24	254	255.255.255.0	0.0.0.255	00000000

	NETWORK	VLAN	VRF	FUNCTION
1				
2				
3				
4				
5				
6				
7				
8				
9				
10				

	FIREWALL / ZONE	SOURCE	DESTINATION	TCP/ UDP
1				
2				
3				
4				
5				
6				
7				
8				
9				
10				

NETWORK

JOURNAL

REFERENCE

CIDR	USABLE IP'S	SUBNET	WILDCARD	BINARY
/30	2	255.255.255.252	0.0.0.3	11111100
/29	6	255.255.255.248	0.0.0.7	11111000
/28	14	255.255.255.240	0.0.0.15	11110000
/27	30	255.255.255.224	0.0.0.31	11100000
/26	62	255.255.255.192	0.0.0.63	11000000
/25	126	255.255.255.128	0.0.0.127	10000000
/24	254	255.255.255.0	0.0.0.255	00000000

	NETWORK	VLAN	VRF	FUNCTION
1				
2				
3				
4				
5				
6				
7				
8				
9				
10				

	FIREWALL / ZONE	SOURCE	DESTINATION	TCP/ UDP
1				
2				
3				
4				
5				
6				
7				
8				
9				
10				

NETWORK JOURNAL

REFERENCE

CIDR	USABLE IP'S	SUBNET	WILDCARD	BINARY
/30	2	255.255.255.252	0.0.0.3	11111100
/29	6	255.255.255.248	0.0.0.7	11111000
/28	14	255.255.255.240	0.0.0.15	11110000
/27	30	255.255.255.224	0.0.0.31	11100000
/26	62	255.255.255.192	0.0.0.63	11000000
/25	126	255.255.255.128	0.0.0.127	10000000
/24	254	255.255.255.0	0.0.0.255	00000000

	NETWORK	VLAN	VRF	FUNCTION
1				
2				
3				
4				
5				
6				
7				
8				
9				
10				

	FIREWALL / ZONE	SOURCE	DESTINATION	TCP/ UDP
1				
2				
3				
4				
5				
6				
7				
8				
9				
10				

NETWORK JOURNAL

REFERENCE

CIDR	USABLE IP'S	SUBNET	WILDCARD	BINARY
/30	2	255.255.255.252	0.0.0.3	11111100
/29	6	255.255.255.248	0.0.0.7	11111000
/28	14	255.255.255.240	0.0.0.15	11110000
/27	30	255.255.255.224	0.0.0.31	11100000
/26	62	255.255.255.192	0.0.0.63	11000000
/25	126	255.255.255.128	0.0.0.127	10000000
/24	254	255.255.255.0	0.0.0.255	00000000

	NETWORK	VLAN	VRF	FUNCTION
1				
2				
3				
4				
5				
6				
7				
8				
9				
10				

	FIREWALL / ZONE	SOURCE	DESTINATION	TCP/ UDP
1				
2				
3				
4				
5				
6				
7				
8				
9				
10				

NETWORK JOURNAL

REFERENCE

CIDR	USABLE IP'S	SUBNET	WILDCARD	BINARY
/30	2	255.255.255.252	0.0.0.3	11111100
/29	6	255.255.255.248	0.0.0.7	11111000
/28	14	255.255.255.240	0.0.0.15	11110000
/27	30	255.255.255.224	0.0.0.31	11100000
/26	62	255.255.255.192	0.0.0.63	11000000
/25	126	255.255.255.128	0.0.0.127	10000000
/24	254	255.255.255.0	0.0.0.255	00000000

	NETWORK	VLAN	VRF	FUNCTION
1				
2				
3				
4				
5				
6				
7				
8				
9				
10				

	FIREWALL / ZONE	SOURCE	DESTINATION	TCP/ UDP
1				
2				
3				
4				
5				
6				
7				
8				
9				
10				

NETWORK ______

JOURNAL

REFERENCE

CIDR	USABLE IP'S	SUBNET	WILDCARD	BINARY
/30	2	255.255.255.252	0.0.0.3	11111100
/29	6	255.255.255.248	0.0.0.7	11111000
/28	14	255.255.255.240	0.0.0.15	11110000
/27	30	255.255.255.224	0.0.0.31	11100000
/26	62	255.255.255.192	0.0.0.63	11000000
/25	126	255.255.255.128	0.0.0.127	10000000
/24	254	255.255.255.0	0.0.0.255	00000000

	NETWORK	VLAN	VRF	FUNCTION
1				
2				
3				
4				
5				
6				
7				
8				
9				
10				

	FIREWALL / ZONE	SOURCE	DESTINATION	TCP/ UDP
1				
2				
3				
4				
5				
6				
7				
8				
9				
10				

ABOUT THE AUTHOR

For the past two decades, I have been providing solutions to a variety of industries and solving complex problems. I am a certified professional in technologies such as Cisco, Check Point, Palo Alto, and VMware, and I have expertise in areas including routers, switches, firewalls, wireless, SD-WAN, Linux, penetration testing and cloud-based solutions.

Email: james@clifford.network

Website: https://clifford.network

LinkedIn: Scan me